MANCHESTER
CITY COUNCIL

KT-174-029

Please return/renew this item
by the last date shown.
Books may also be renewed by
phone or the internet.

Tel: 0161 254 7777

www.manchester.gov.uk/libraries

SIMON

Published in 2023 by Welbeck Children's Limited
part of the Welbeck Publishing Group
Based in London and Sydney
www.welbeckpublishing.com
Text © 2023 Simon Mugford
Design & Illustration © 2023 Dan Green
ISBN: 978-1-78312-976-8

Writer: Simon Mugford
Designer and Illustrator: Dan Green
Design Manager: Sam James
Commissioning Editor: Suhel Ahmed
Production: Arlene Alexander
Research Assistant: Eleanor Reid

A catalogue record for this book is available from the British Library.

Printed in the UK
10 9 8 7 6 5 4 3 2 1

Statistics and records correct as of December 2022

FOOTBALL SUPERSTARS

FOOTBALL RULES THE WORLD

SIMON MUGFORD   DAN GREEN

CONTENTS

INTRODUCTION

Are you one of the **BILLIONS** of people in the world who loves the world's **NUMBER ONE** sport?

If you are, then this is **DEFINITELY** the book for you!

FOOTBALL RULES THE WORLD brings you the most incredible stories about the **BIGGEST GAME** on the planet . . .

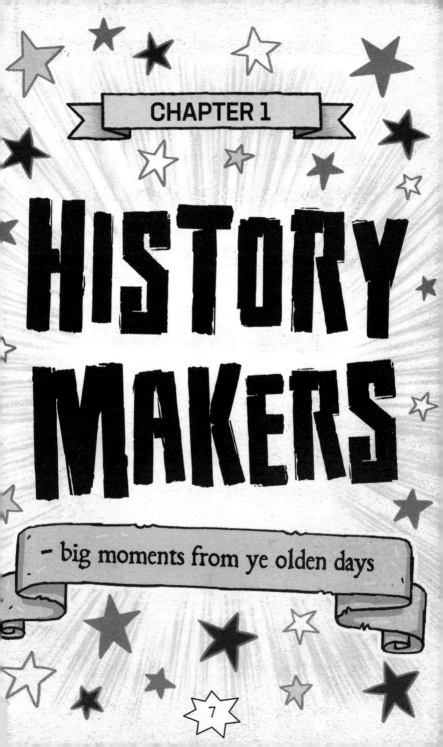

CHAPTER 1

HISTORY MAKERS

- big moments from ye olden days

THE CHRISTMAS TRUCE

25 December 1914 - the first Christmas of **World War I.** On that day, so it is said, thousands of British and German soldiers called a truce and the fighting stopped.

Instead, they shared food and drink, told jokes ... and **played football** in the mud.

There are stories of an organised match, which the Germans won **3–2,** but the history books say this probably didn't happen.

But even if the soldiers only played kickabouts, it shows that sometimes - football is so much **more than a game.**

LEGENDARY LADIES

Dick, Kerr Ladies was a women's football team from **Preston, England.** They were formed at a factory in 1917 and played against both men's and women's teams.

The team gained a **huge following,** and in 1920, they played St Helen's Ladies in front of **53,000 fans** at Everton's Goodison Park.

This record crowd for a women's game stood for **98 years.**

It was a **charity match,** to raise money for **injured soldiers** returning from the First World War. The Dick, Kerr Ladies won the match **4–0!**

A year later, the English **FA BANNED** women from playing football!

UNBELIEVABLE!

READ MORE ABOUT THIS ON **PAGE 46**

11

THE 1950 WORLD CUP 'FINAL'

The deciding match of the **1950 World Cup** saw tournament hosts **Brazil** (the favourites) play their South American rivals **Uruguay**.

Instead of *TWO* teams in a final, *FOUR* teams played a final group stage. This was the last match for both teams. Yes — *it's weird.*

The match was played at the famous Maracana Stadium in Rio de Janeiro. Officially, **173,850 fans** came to watch, but it's said there were up to **220,000.**

Brazil stormed through the tournament and they were the runaway favourites. But guess what? **Uruguay won . . . 2–1**

ALCIDES GHIGGIA

This was Uruguay's **second** World Cup win – they had won the **first** ever tournament in **1930**.

PELE RULES!

NAME: Edson Arantes do Nascimento

DATE OF BIRTH: 23 October 1940

NATIONAL TEAM: Brazil

CLUBS: Santos, New York Cosmos

POSITION: Forward

*More commonly known as Pele, **the 17-year-old** wonderkid scored a hat-trick for Brazil in the semi-final of the 1958 World Cup. In the final, he scored two **SENSATIONAL** goals to bring Brazil their first **World Cup**.*

A legend was born . . .

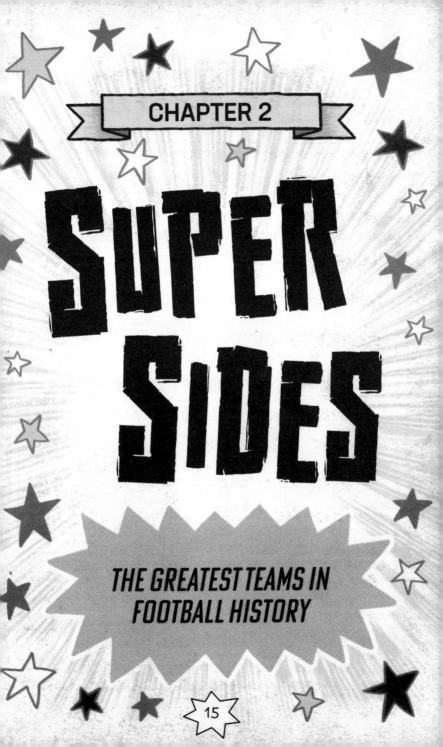

CHAPTER 2

SUPER SIDES

THE GREATEST TEAMS IN FOOTBALL HISTORY

BRAZIL 1970

The **Brazil** team that won the **1970 World Cup** in Mexico is often said to be the best ever.

Carlos Alberto, Tostao, Rivelino, Jairzinho, and, of course, **Pele** are some of the legendary names in a side famous for their beautiful, attacking football.

CARLOS ALBERTO

TOSTAO

RIVELINO

JAIRZINHO

PELE

Jairzinho scored in every Brazil game in Mexico.

Nicknamed The *Selecao*, Brazil beat every team they played at the tournament, including reigning champions **England**, to reach the final where they beat **Italy** 4-1.

It was Pele's **THIRD** World Cup win - the only player ever to do it.

Read about Carlos Alberto's famous goal in the final on page 76

LIVERPOOL 1983-84

This Liverpool side made history as they became the first English team to win a **TREBLE:**

The **LEAGUE** title (for the **15th** time)

The **League Cup** (beat local rivals Everton in the final)

The
Milk Cup

Their **FOURTH EUROPEAN CUP**

Striker **Ian Rush** scored an awesome **47 goals** in all competitions in that season.

MANCHESTER UNITED
1998-99

Led by manager **Alex Ferguson**, this United team, which included **David Beckham, Roy Keane** and **Ole Gunnar Solksjaer**, are the **only** English side to win the treble of the **Premier League, FA Cup** and **Champions League**.

ALEX FERGUSON

SEE PAGE 60

The team went unbeaten in **33** games and the Champions League final against **Bayern Munich** is one of the most famous games in history.

19

DAVID BECKHAM

THE GALACTICOS

Starting in 2000, **Real Madrid** signed some of the finest, **MOST EXPENSIVE** footballers in the world. They were known as the **GALACTICOS** and included:

LUIS FIGO, *WINGER*
€62 MILLION

ZINEDINE ZIDANE, *MIDFIELDER*
€73.5 MILLION

RONALDO, *STRIKER*
€45 MILLION

DAVID BECKHAM, *WINGER*
€37.5 MILLION

KAKA, *MIDFIELDER*
€67 MILLION

KARIM BENZEMA, *STRIKER*
€30 MILLION

CRISTIANO RONALDO, *FORWARD*
€94 MILLION

LUKA MODRIC, *MIDFELDER*
€32 MILLION

GARETH BALE, *WINGER*
€100 MILLION

NETHERLANDS 1974

This Dutch side played a system called **TOTAL FOOTBALL,** where each outfield player in the side, including the genius **Johan Cruyff,** would play in any position. It was quick, clever and brilliant to watch.

The team beat both **Argentina** and **Brazil** at the **1974 World Cup** but were ultimately beaten by a ruthless **West Germany.**

BARCELONA 2008-09

PEP GUARDIOLA

Manager **Pep Guardiola** brought his own version of **Total Football** to Barcelona. The star-studded side, including **Lionel Messi, Samuel Eto'o, Xavi** and **Andres Iniesta** passed the ball and moved quickly - they called it **TIKI TAKA.**

It worked - Pep led Barca to the **TREBLE** in his first season in charge and a total of **14 TROPHIES** in four seasons.

KA-POW!

MESSI RULES!

NAME: Lionel Andres Messi Cuccittini

DATE OF BIRTH: 24 June 1987

NATIONAL TEAM: Argentina

CLUBS: Barcelona, Paris Saint Germain

POSITION: Forward

At Barcelona from the ages of 13 to 33 Messi won La Liga **TEN** times and the Champions League **FOUR** times, as well as the **Ballon d'Or** a record **SEVEN** times. Known by many as the G.O.A.T (Greatest of All Time) Messi is the most gifted player of his generation.

CHAPTER 3

UNDERDOGS AND UPSETS

SHOCK WINS AND GIANT-KILLERS

DANES CRASH THE EUROS

When Yugoslavia were expelled from **EURO 1992** because of a war, **Denmark** were the last-minute replacement.

After finishing ahead of **England** and **France** in their group, Denmark beat reigning champions the **Netherlands** on penalties in the semi-final.

Their 2-0 win over **Germany** in the final **STUNNED** the world of football.

Probably the best tournament upset in the world!

SAUDIS SHOCK ARGENTINA

Argentina began the **2022 World Cup** as one of the favourites. Unbeaten in 32 matches and led by the magic of Messi, they opened their tournament against **Saudi Arabia** (ranked 51 in the world).

Argentina went ahead with a Messi penalty early on, but in the second half... the Saudis scored TWO quick goals to produce a **WORLD CUP SHOCKER!**

Despite this shock upset, **Argentina** went on to **win** the tournament! (see page 70)

FOXES RULE!

Leicester City were almost relegated from the **Premier League** in 2015 and began the next season as favourites to go down. But . . .

With a team of unlikely stars, including former non-league striker **Jamie Vardy,** their Premier League win in 2016 is one one of the greatest upsets in all sport – not just football.

BOP!

Match of the Day host - and Leicester fan - **Gary Lineker** promised he would present the show in his boxer shorts if Leicester won the league - and he did!

PANTS!

VIKINGS SLAY ENGLAND

What happened when the stars of **England** came up against **Iceland** (ranked 34 in the world at the time) at **EURO 2016?**

England went ahead with an early penalty, but the Icelanders took advantage of a terribly **disappointing team** and won **2-1.**

SKOL!

WIGAN STUN CITY

With superstars like **Sergio Aguero** and **Yaya Toure** in their team, City were firm favourites to beat Wigan in the **2013 FA Cup Final.**

AGUERO

TOURE

BOF!

With City down to ten men, Wigan's **Ben Watson** headed in a 91st-minute winner.

UNBELIEVABLE SCENES!

The following week, Wigan were relegated from the Premier League.

JOY FOR JAPAN

In March 2011, Japan was struck by a terrible **tsunami** that killed thousands of people. So the people at home did not pay much attention to their women's team at the **World Cup** in Germany - they had bigger things to think about.

A **MAGNITUDE 9** EARTHQUAKE HAS STRUCK JAPAN.

NEWS

DISASTER!

WORLD NEWS
LIVE

But the team were **AWESOME** and against the odds, they reached the final. After a tight 2-2 draw, Japan beat the **world's best team** - the **USA** - on penalties. It was a major upset and fantastic for the people of Japan.

Japan's **Homare Sawa** won the **Golden Boot** for being top scorer and the **Golden Ball** for best player.

HENRY RULES!

NAME: Thierry Daniel Henry

DATE OF BIRTH: 17 August 1977

NATIONAL TEAM: France

CLUBS: Monaco, Juventus, Arsenal, Barcelona, New York Red Bulls

POSITION: Striker

*Arsenal's all-time **top scorer** and Premier League legend, **treble-winner** with Barcelona and a **World Cup** and **EUROs** winner with France, Thierry Henry is one of the finest strikers ever to play the game.*

CHAPTER 4

MEGA MANAGERS

THE BEST BRAINS IN THE GAME

SIR ALEX FERGUSON

'Fergie' led **Manchester United** for an astonishing 27 years. He made stars out of youth team players such as **David Beckham** and **Paul Scholes,** and signed major talents, including **Roy Keane** and **Cristiano Ronaldo** to bring unmatched success to United. He's probably the greatest manager of all time.

13 x PREMIER LEAGUE TITLES

5 x FA CUPS

2 x CHAMPIONS LEAGUE TITLES

SHANKLY AND *PAISLEY*

In the 1960s, **Bill Shankly** transformed **Liverpool** from Second Division no-hopers to **three-time** First Division champions, FA Cup and UEFA Cup winners.

BILL SHANKLY

BOB PAISLEY

Shankly's assistant **Bob Paisley** took over in 1974 and won **SIX** more league titles and **THREE** European Cups. **Liverpool legends.**

BRIAN CLOUGH

Clough led **Derby County** to a First Division title in 1972, then did the same at **Nottingham Forest** in 1978, having just got them promoted. But that's not all . . .

Having qualified for the **European Cup,** Clough's Forest **WON** it back-to-back in **1979** and **1980**.

In 1979 Clough famously signed Britain's first **£1 MILLION player – Trevor Francis.**

"I WOULDN'T SAY I WAS THE BEST MANAGER IN THE BUSINESS. BUT I WAS IN THE **TOP ONE.**"

ARSENE WENGER

In 22 years as **Arsenal** manager, Wenger won seven **FA Cups** and three **Premier League** titles, including the **DOUBLE** twice.

Wenger's 'scientific' approach to football earned him the nickname 'Le Prof' and his influence on modern football is **MASSIVE.**

CARLO ANCELOTTI

It takes a lot to beat **'Don Carlo'**. He's won FOUR **Champions Leagues** as a manager - more than anyone else - and is the only boss to win each of Europe's **top five** leagues.

OTTO REHHAGEL

An underdog specialist, Rehhagel twice won the **Bundesliga** with **Werder Bremen** and

then with **Kaiserslautern** - having just won promotion! But his shock triumph - winning **EURO 2004** with Greece - surely tops the lot.

SIR ALF RAMSEY

Tractor Boys forever!

Ramsey won **Ipswich Town** promotion from the old **Second Division** in 1961. Incredibly, the Suffolk club were English champions the following season and Ramsey left to manage **England.**

Winning the **1966 World Cup** makes Sir Alf Ramsey one of the most celebrated English managers of all time.

JURGEN KLOPP

Klopp's style of exciting, attacking football has won Liverpool both the **Champions League** and the **Premier League** and a new generation of fans. A modern-day master.

SARINA WIEGMAN

By leading the England women's team to victory in **EURO 22**, she's won a place in the heart of every England fan.

BEST RULES!

NAME: George Best

DATE OF BIRTH: 22 May 1946

NATIONAL TEAM: Northern Ireland

CLUBS: Manchester United *(and many others, including Fulham)*

POSITION: Winger, attacking midfielder

*Famous for his long hair and cool clothes, Best was the original **fashionable footballer**. The **Manchester United** star of the 1960s and 70s was the most **dazzling** player of the time – with his dribbling, passing – and scoring skills he was **unstoppable**.*

CHAPTER 5

WOMEN RULE

FREE TO PLAY

Despite the success of the sport, especially in the late **1910s**, the FA believed that football was bad for women - no one knows why - so women's football was officially **BANNED** from **1921** to **1970**. It was also banned in **Brazil** and **Germany**.

In England, **Southampton Women** won the

first women's **FA Cup Final** in **1971**. Their star player, **Pat 'Thunder' Davies** scored a hat-trick as they beat **Stewarton Thistle** 4-1.

Southampton would go on to win the FA Cup **seven** more times.

Davies was later selected for England Women when they played their first international match against **Scotland** in 1972.

GO USA!

The first **FIFA Women's World Cup** was held in China in **1991.** It was won by the **USA** – and they went on to win again in **1999, 2015** and **2019.** They have produced some of the **BIGGEST** names in women's football.

MIA HAMM

POSITION: **FORWARD**

YEARS: **1989-2004**

158 goals in **276 games**

MEGAN RAPINOE

POSITION: **MIDFIELDER**

YEARS: **2005-PRESENT**

Ballon d'Or winner **2019**

CARLI LLOYD

POSITION: **FORWARD**

YEARS: **1999-2021**

Scored a famous **hat-trick** in the **2015** World Cup final

49

WONDER WOMEN

Here are some more star names in the women's game to look out for:

SAM KERR

COUNTRY: **AUSTRALIA**

POSITION: **FORWARD**

YEARS: **2008-PRESENT**

Golden Boot winner in three different leagues

All-time top scorer in the USA's NWSL

Kerr is the only Australian – male or female – to score a **World Cup** hat-trick.

WENDIE RENARD

COUNTRY: **FRANCE**

POSITION: **DEFENDER**

YEARS: **2006-PRESENT**

Won 14 French League titles

Won SEVEN Champions League titles

ALEXIA PUTELLAS

COUNTRY: **SPAIN**

POSITION: **MIDFIELDER / WINGER**

YEARS: **2010-PRESENT**

Won a TREBLE with Barcelona in 2021

Voted FIFA Best Player in 2021

LIONESSES RULE!

England was the host nation for **Women's EURO 2022.** The year before, the men's team had reached a EUROs final **for the first time** - but failed to win. Could the **Lionesses** beat that?

England faced **Germany** (who else?) in the final at Wembley. **Ella Toone** put England ahead, only for Germany to equalise and send the match to extra time.

BOOM!

The attendance was **87,192** - a record EUROs crowd for men or women.

Chloe Kelly wrote herself into the history books with her 110th-minute goal as England won **2–1.**

INCREDIBLE!

YES!

17.6 MILLION fans watched the match on TV.

LIONESS LEGENDS

The 2022 England win made the players household names, such as:

LEAH WILLIAMSON

POSITION: **MIDFIELD/CENTRE-BACK**

CLUB: **ARSENAL**

England's awesome captain

CHLOE KELLY

POSITION: **STRIKER**

CLUB: **MANCHESTER CITY**

Scored the winner in the EURO 2022 final

BETH MEAD

POSITION: **FORWARD**

CLUB: **ARSENAL**

Won the Golden Boot at EURO 2022

ALESSIA RUSSO

POSITION: **FORWARD**

CLUB: **MANCHESTER UNITED**

Scored a superb back-heel goal in the EURO 2022 semi-final

PARR RULES!

NAME: Lily Parr

DATE OF BIRTH: 26 April 1905

NATIONALITY: English

CLUBS: St Helens Ladies, Dick, Kerr Ladies

POSITION: Forward

*Parr was a true trailblazer, a **legend** in the history of the women's game. Playing for more than 30 years for the famous club **Dick, Kerr Ladies**, Parr had a very powerful left foot and is said to have scored more than **900 goals!***

CHAPTER 6

THE BIG GAME

MOST MEMORABLE MATCHES
FROM HISTORY

23 JULY 1966

WORLD CUP QUARTER-FINAL

PORTUGAL 5-3 NORTH KOREA

GOODISON PARK

North Korea had already produced the shock of the tournament – beating **Italy 1–0** in the group stage. Now they faced a **Portugal** side with the great **Eusebio** in the quarter-final.

Incredibly, North Korea went ahead just after **KICK-OFF**, and were 3-0 up after just 25 minutes!

BOOM!

Eusebio suddenly took charge, scoring FOUR GOALS - including two penalties - before **Jose Augusto** made it five.

UNBELIEVABLE!

17 JUNE 1970

WORLD CUP SEMI-FINAL

ITALY 4-3 WEST GERMANY (AET)

AZTEC STADIUM, MEXICO CITY

More than **100,000** fans had gathered in the heat of **Mexico City** to watch two footballing giants.

Italy led early on, only for **West Germany** to equalise in stoppage time. What followed was the most extraordinary extra time ever:

94 MINUTES: *GERMANY GOAL* **1·2**

98 MINUTES: *ITALY GOAL* **2·2**

104 MINUTES: ITALY GOAL **3-2**

110 MINUTES: GERMANY GOAL **3-3**

111 MINUTES: ITALY GOAL **4-3**

Five extra-time goals, both teams exhausted.

Fans had just witnessed

THE **GAME** OF THE **CENTURY.**

MEXICO 70

PHEW, I'M EXHAUSTED!

26 MAY 1989

FIRST DIVISION

LIVERPOOL 0-2 ARSENAL

ANFIELD STADIUM

Liverpool were three points ahead of **Arsenal** going into this game - the **First Division** decider. Liverpool were the title holders and had just won the **FA CUP** - they were THE team to beat. Arsenal needed to win by **TWO** clear goals to clinch the league on goal difference.

The *First Division* became the *Premier League* in 1992. This is the old trophy.

Arsenal went **1–0** up early in the second half thanks to Alan Smith's header. The tension was ridiculous . . . right up until Michael Thomas grabbed a **91st-MINUTE** winner. **MAYHEM.** The Arsenal fans went wild! It was one of the greatest moments in Arsenal's history.

MICHAEL THOMAS

BOOM!

26 MAY 1999

CHAMPIONS LEAGUE FINAL

MANCHESTER UNITED 2-1 BAYERN MUNICH

NOU CAMP, BARCELONA

Both teams went into this match as league champions. Manchester United were also FA cup winners. Win this and they would claim a **TREBLE**.

LET'S DO THIS!

Bayern Munich were ahead after just **SIX MINUTES**. United couldn't break through until . . . David Beckham's **stoppage-time** corner found sub **Teddy Sheringham** . . .

GOAL! 1-1! Game on.

Instantly, United had another corner . . . **Ole Gunnar Solksjaer** (also a sub) was there to score!

UNITED WON 2-1!

The Bayern players were broken - while the United players and fans were in dreamland.

BLAM!

25 MAY 2005

CHAMPIONS LEAGUE FINAL

AC MILAN 3-3 LIVERPOOL (AET)

ATATURK STADIUM, ISTANBUL

Liverpool were the underdogs against a peak **AC Milan**. And the Italian side went ahead in under a minute. By half-time, Liverpool were losing 3-0 and it looked to be all over for **The Reds**.

POW!

But something incredible happened in the second-half. Thanks to goals from **Steven Gerrard**, **Vladimir Smicer** and **Xabi Alonso**, Liverpool made it 3-3, forcing extra-time and a penalty shoot-out.

VLADIMIR SMICER

STEVEN GERRARD

XABI ALONSO

Liverpool keeper Jerzy Dudek was the hero as they won the shoot-out to cap an incredible comeback –

THE MIRACLE OF ISTANBUL.

The opening game of the tournament saw host nation **Angola** go into half-time leading **2-0** thanks to their striker **Flavio.**

They extended their lead to **4-0** in the second half, only for Mali's **Seydou Keita** and **Frederic Kanoute** to get Mali back in the game. It was **4-2** in the 90th minute, but then . . .

FREDERIC KANOUTE

Keita and **Mustapha Yatabare** added TWO more in injury time to produce a stunning fightback.

4-4!

YES!

MUSTAPHA YATABARE

18 DECEMBER 2022

WORLD CUP FINAL

ARGENTINA 3-3 FRANCE *(4-2 on penalties)*

LUSAIL STADIUM, QATAR

The holders France faced tournament favourites **Argentina** in what was billed as a showdown between **Lionel Messi** and **Kylian Mbappe.** And what a match it was!

Argentina dominated for **80 minutes** with a 2-0 lead. Then in a breathtaking final 10 minutes, **Mbappe** scored from the spot and quickly equalised with an incredible volley to force extra-time.

Messi restored Argentina's lead, only for Mbappe's late penalty to take the game to the shoot-out, where the South Americans prevailed. **INCREDIBLE** scenes!

It was hailed as the

GREATEST WORLD CUP FINAL – EVER!

BECKHAM RULES!

NAME: David Robert Joseph Beckham

DATE OF BIRTH: 2 May 1975

NATIONAL TEAM: England

CLUBS: Manchester United, Preston North End (loan), Real Madrid, LA Galaxy, AC Milan (loan), Paris Saint-Germain

POSITION: Midfielder

*Probably the finest midfielder of his generation and known for his incredible **bending crosses** and **free-kicks**, Beckham won **19** major trophies, mostly with **Manchester United** and his fame extends way beyond the game.*

CHAPTER 7

GOAL-DEN GOALS

SOME OF THE GREATEST GOALS EVER SCORED

THE **GOAL** OF THE **CENTURY**

22 JUNE 1986   ARGENTINA 2-1 ENGLAND

The **1986 World Cup** quarter-final between England and Argentina that ended 2-1 to Argentina is remembered for **TWO GOALS** by Diego Maradona.

THAT'S HANDY!

Maradona is *hands down* one of the greatest ever players.

Even *hands up!*

Just **four minutes** after the ref missed his **handball** goal (the 'Hand of God') and left England reeling, Maradona started a run in his own half. He swept past FOUR England players before sending keeper Peter Shilton the wrong way to score the *GOAL OF THE CENTURY.*

THE GOAL THAT MADE
BRAZIL

21 JUNE 1970   BRAZIL 4-1 ITALY

The Brazil team that won the **1970 World Cup** was one of the **greatest** of all time.

The **fourth goal** in their **4–1** win over **Italy** was the finest example of their greatness.

KA-POW!

Brazil began a move in their own half, dribbling past the Italians and eventually finding their star forward **Pele.**

Captain **Carlos Alberto** had started a run down the right and when Pele's perfect pass found him, he struck it brilliantly -*BOOM.*

ZOOM!

THE BEAUTIFUL GAME HAD ARRIVED!

MESSI'S MARADONA MOMENT

18 APRIL 2007
BARCELONA 5-2 GETAFE

Back in **2007**, Barcelona's Lionel Messi was yet to become the legend we know. This goal, against **Getafe** in the **Copa Del Rey** semi-final, was *almost identical* to Maradona's Goal of the Century.

Messi picked up the ball *in his own half* and then dribbled past two players. Running at speed with the ball at his feet, he **zipped and turned** his way through three more opponents, and rounded the keeper to score.

WHAM!

AN INCREDIBLE SOLO GOAL.

Barcelona's fans voted this as the **BEST EVER** Barcelona goal.

ROONEY BIKES BACK

12 FEBRUARY 2011
MANCHESTER UNITED 2-1 MANCHESTER CITY

A bicycle-kick goal impresses on any occasion, but in the **Manchester Derby** it's sensational.

Wayne Rooney's 2011 effort against City was one of the best – and most **spectacular** – Premier League goals on record.

BLAM!

ZLATAN SINKS ENGLAND

14 NOVEMBER 2012 SWEDEN 4-2 ENGLAND

Sweden's **Zlatan Ibrahimovic** was already on a hat-trick, when from **way outside the box** and with his back to goal, his acrobatic **bicycle kick** sent the ball flying into the **England** net.

TAKE ZLAT!

RONALDO'S PORTO PILEDRIVER

15 APRIL 2009   PORTO 0-1 MANCHESTER UNITED

In **2009**, **Manchester United** were in Portugal, playing **Porto** away in the **Champions League** quarter-final. United needed to win or they would be out of the competition. **Six** minutes into the game, Cristiano Ronaldo picked up a pass from **40** yards out and **fired . . .**

WHOMP!

It was a real screamer, flying at **64.2 mph** . . . and . . .

GOAAAAAAL!

The Porto keeper had **no chance!**

THIS WAS THE **BEST** GOAL I EVER SCORED!

RONALDO RULES!

NAME: Cristiano Ronaldo dos Santos Aveiro

DATE OF BIRTH: 5 February 1985

NATIONAL TEAM: Portugal

CLUBS: Sporting Lisbon, Manchester United (2003-2009), Real Madrid, Juventus, Manchester United (2021-2022), Al Nassr

POSITION: Forward/left winger

The stats tell you everything about Cristiano Ronaldo. The **five-times Champions League** winner has more **goals, appearances and assists** in the competition than any other player and the most international goals. He says he is the greatest of all time. Can you argue with that?

CHAPTER 8

GAME CHANGERS

THE PLAYERS THAT HAVE MADE A DIFFERENCE ON – AND OFF – THE PITCH

BREAKING *BARRIERS*

Arthur Wharton is thought to be the **world's first black professional footballer.** Back in the **1880s**, this sporting wonder (Arthur was also a track athlete and the fastest man in Britain) played as a goalkeeper and a winger for teams including **Preston North End** and **Sheffield United**.

In **1925**, Plymouth Argyle's **Jack Leslie** became the first black player to be selected for England. But when the FA realised he was black, they stopped him playing. **Unbelievable!**

Jack was finally awarded his cap in 2022, **34 years** after his death.

It wasn't until **1978** that England had its first full international black player - defender **Viv Anderson.**

Andrew Watson, who played for **Scotland** in the **1880s**, is thought to be the first black footballer to play internationally.

87

MAGIC MARCUS

In 2020, **Marcus Rashford** was best known as a brilliant forward for **Manchester United** and England.

But that all changed during the **Coronavirus pandemic.** When the British government planned to stop giving poorer families help with food vouchers, **Marcus spoke out.**

Remembering his own childhood, when his **family struggled for money,** Rashford started a campaign asking the government to change its mind.

Social media lit up with love for Rashford. He was a footballer **AND** an **activist** – a national hero, too!

PITCHING **IN**

Bayern Munich's **Sadio Mane** has never forgotten his home village of **Bambali** in **Senegal.** He has paid for a school and hospital there and regularly sends money to every family in the village.

Former Chelsea legend **Didier Drogba** has a charity that helps children in his home country of **Ivory Coast.**

90

Mario Balotelli is known for some crazy antics on and off the pitch, but he's famously funded causes from **homelessness** to **animal charities**.

The one and only **Zlatan Ibrahimovic** gave money to fight **Coronavirus** in Italy.

"IF THE VIRUS DON'T GO TO ZLATAN, ZLATAN GOES TO THE VIRUS!"

UH-OH!

POWER PLAY

From the 1980s until the early 2000s, **George Weah** played as striker for top European clubs including **Monaco, PSG, AC Milan**, and **Chelsea**. Weah was one of the great players of the time and won the **Ballon d'Or** in 1995.

BALLON D'OR

His home country **Liberia,** in West Africa, suffered years of war and terrible poverty. At first, Weah worked with **children's charities** and the **United Nations**, which led him into politics . . .

. . . and George Weah has been the **PRESIDENT** of Liberia since 2018.

A GREAT HONOUR!

THE **GOD** OF **NAPLES**

In **1984,** the great Argentine player **Diego Maradona** joined **Napoli** in the southern Italian city of **Naples.** It was very poor compared to the northern Italian cities, where clubs such as **Juventus** and **AC Milan** dominated Serie A. Naples were lucky to avoid relegation.

Maradona changed that. He led Napoli to their **FIRST EVER** Serie A title in **1987**, another in **1990**, the **Coppa Italia** and the **UEFA CUP**.

UEFA CUP

THE GOD OF NAPLES

Maradona grew up poor - and for the people of Naples - he was one of their own. They **WORSHIPPED** him.

KING ERIC

Eric Cantona was a Premier League legend at **Manchester United,** but he was famously often in trouble. **Banned** from football for kung fu-kicking a Crystal Palace fan in **1995**, his **bad boy** style made him famous outside of football.

Cantona went on to become an actor!

GAZZA'S TEARS

When **Paul Gascoigne** received a yellow card in the **1990 World Cup** semi-final between **England** and **West Germany,** he started crying as it meant he would miss the final if England went through.

His tearful reaction melted hearts around the world and he became one of the most **famous** people on the planet . . .

SNIFF!

But England lost on penalties . . .

THE **QUEEN** OF SOCCER

Marta is the arguably the greatest female player of all time - **Pele** himself named his fellow Brazilian **'Pele in skirts'**. Marta has scored more **World Cup** goals - 17 - than any player, male or female, and her superb skill has won her **SIX** FIFA World Player of the Year Awards.

PIONEERING *POWELL*

Hope Powell was a pioneering women's player in the 1980s and 90s before becoming the **FIRST EVER** full-time coach of the **England Women's team.** Having led England to the final of **EURO 2009,** Hope paved the way for the successful **Lionesses** today.

RONALDO RULES!

NAME: Ronaldo Luis Nazario de Lima

DATE OF BIRTH: 18 September 1976

NATIONAL TEAM: Brazil

CLUBS: Cruzeiro, PSV Eindhoven, Barcelona, Inter Milan, Real Madrid, AC Milan, Corinthians

POSITION: Striker

*Known as **The Phenomenon,** Ronaldo's style of playing up front - starting an attack deep and dribbling at pace - was a massive influence on today's strikers. At his best, there were few strikers better than Ronaldo.*

CHAPTER 9

CLUB TOGETHER

THE SIDES THAT DO THINGS DIFFERENTLY

THE **GREEN** TEAM

The **GREEN** in **Forest Green Rovers** is more than just a name. It is the world's most environmentally friendly club.

The **English League One** club is the only **VEGAN** club in the world. All the pies sold there are vegan and the players take vegan packed lunches to away games.

GREEN POWER!

Nom, nom!

Their **organic pitch** is watered with **recycled rain** and **waste water** and the team travel in an **electric coach**.

WHIZZ!

BEEP! BEEP!

ELECTROBUS

Barcelona defender and former Arsenal player **Hector Bellerin** is a major investor in the club.

HECTOR IS VEGAN

THANKS HECTOR!

THE FOOTBALL ANARCHISTS

St Pauli is a club in **Hamburg, Germany.**
Their record on the pitch is unremarkable,
yo-yoing between the **Bundesliga** and the
German **second tier.**

But it's the **fans** that make the club stand out . . .

Since the **1980s,** St Pauli has had a 'cult' following of fans from the alternative scene of **punks**, **squatters** and **radicals** in their city.

With their adopted skull and crossbones flag, the St Pauli fans fight **AGAINST** fascist football hooligans but **FOR** social justice.

But still have a good time doing it!

EQUALITY RULES

Lewes FC, in West Sussex, England is a club that likes to do things differently. For 'The Rooks', **community** and **equality** comes first. Locals and fans are encouraged to own a stake in the club where **pride** and **passion** is more important than **profit**.

Most importantly, Lewes is the first club in the world where the **men's** and **women's** teams are **truly equal,** playing with the same resources, funding, facilities and support.

And their ticket sales, sponsorship and performances are doing better as a result.

FANS FIRST

In **Germany,** football clubs must be partly owned by their fans. It's the **LAW! Bayern Munich** - the biggest German club of all - is **75 per cent-owned** by its **supporters.** Ticket prices are low and the fans have a say in how the club is run.

BRILLIANT!

STAR POWER

In the 1970s, US club **NEW YORK COSMOS** signed global superstars such as **Franz Beckenbauer** and **Pele.** The team suddenly became world famous, giving football (or 'soccer' in American) a boost in the USA. The team were more like **rock stars** than footballers!

CUTTING EDGE

MLS side **Portland Timbers** have a VERY **unusual** way of celebrating a goal at their home stadium. The club mascot is a real-life **lumberjack, TIMBER JOEY.** When the Timbers score, Joey **CHAINSAWS** a piece of wood from a tree trunk for the player to hold.

CRUYFF RULES!

NAME: Hendrik Johannes Cruyff

DATE OF BIRTH: 25 April 1947

NATIONAL TEAM: Netherlands

CLUBS: Ajax, Barcelona, LA Aztecs, Washington Diplomats, Levante, Ajax, Feyenoord

POSITION: Forward/attacking midfielder

*Three-times Ballon d'Or winner Johan Cruyff was the Dutch master of **TOTAL FOOTBALL,** the style of technical passing, movement and positioning that revolutionised the modern game.*

*He is famous for the **Cruyff Turn** - faking a pass or shot before dragging the ball behind your standing leg - **genius!***

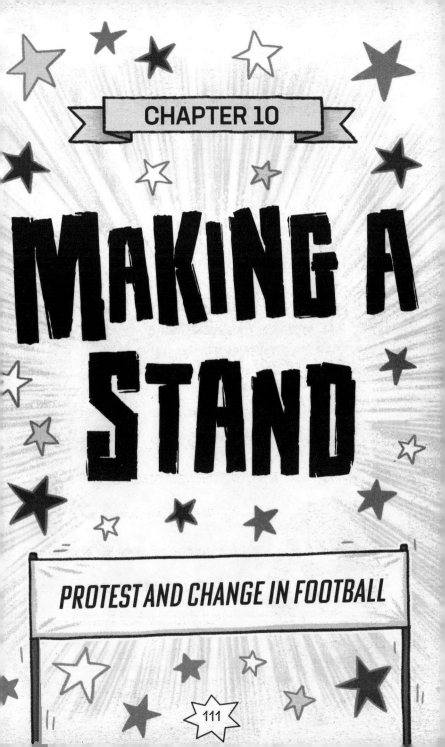

CHAPTER 10

MAKING A STAND

PROTEST AND CHANGE IN FOOTBALL

KICKING **RACISM** OUT

Football clubs, players and fans around the world have played their part in speaking out **against racism** and other forms of **discrimination**.

The **KICK IT OUT** campaign led the way, starting in England in the 1990s.

Now, many teams choose to **take the knee** in a show of togetherness before kick-off.

WORLD CUP OF CONTROVERSY

The **2022 World Cup** in **Qatar** became known for much more than football.

When **FIFA** told teams they could not wear a **ONE LOVE armband,** which promoted inclusion, the German football team protested...

FAIR **PAY**, FAIR **PLAY**

ALEX MORGAN

MEGAN RAPINOE

In 2016, players from the **US Women's National Team** including Alex Morgan, Megan Rapinoe and Carli Lloyd began a campaign to bring equal pay and funding to the men's and women's teams. In 2021, the **GOALS act** was passed, doing just that.

GOALS ACT

From **2022,** all players of both USA teams will receive the **same pay** for appearances, tournament victories and **equal and fair** distribution of World Cup **prize money.**

CARLI LLOYD

ZIDANE RULES!

NAME: Zinedine Yazid Zidane

DATE OF BIRTH: 23 June 1972

NATIONAL TEAM: France

CLUBS: Cannes, Bordeaux, Juventus, Real Madrid

POSITION: Attacking midfielder

'Zizou' is one of the greatest No.10s ever to play football. **Elegant** and **stylish,** Zidane played with a vision and technique like few others. A winner of multiple titles and awards including the **World Cup**, **Ballon d'Or** and the **Champions League,** Zidane went on to be a hugely successful manager at **Real Madrid.**

TOP OF THE SHOTS

ALL-TIME TOP GOALSCORER

PELE (BRAZIL)

1,283 GOALS, **1,384** GAMES

TOP INTERNATIONAL GOALSCORER (WOMEN)

CHRISTINE SINCLAIR (CANADA)

190 GOALS, **310** CAPS

TOP INTERNATIONAL SCORER (MEN)

CRISTIANO RONALDO (PORTUGAL)

118 GOALS, **196** CAPS

MOST GOALS IN A CALENDAR YEAR (MEN)
LIONEL MESSI (ARGENTINA)
91 GOALS IN 2012

MOST INTERNATIONAL CAPS (WOMEN)
KRISTINE LILLY (USA)
354 CAPS

WORLD CUP ALL-TIME TOP GOALSCORER
(MEN AND WOMEN)
MARTA (BRAZIL)
17 GOALS IN **5** TOURNAMENTS

QUIZ TIME!

How much do you know about **FOOTBALL?** Try this quiz to find out, then test your friends!

1. Which team won the first ever World Cup in 1930?

Uruguay

2. When did Manchester United win the TREBLE?

1998/99

3. Which national side played TOTAL FOOTBALL?

Netherlands

4. Which team won EURO 1992?

denmaxrk

5. Which team shocked Argentina with a 2-1 win at the 2022 World Cup?

Svodiarbia

6. When was the first Women's World Cup held?

1991

---

7. Which player scored the 'Goal of the Century' in 1986?

Diego maradona

---

8. Who is thought to be the first black professional footballer?

arther whaxtorn

---

9. Which football club is the first in the world to pay men and women the same?

Lewes FC

---

10. What is the Portland Timbers mascot called?

Timber Joey

The answers are on the next page *but no peeking!*

ANSWERS

1. Uruguay

2. 1998/99

3. Netherlands

4. Denmark

5. Saudi Arabia

6. 1991

7. Diego Maradona

8. Arthur Wharton

9. Lewes FC

10. Timber Joey

FOOTBALL WORDS
YOU SHOULD KNOW

World Cup
The biggest tournament for international teams.

Ballon d'Or
The award for the year's best footballer in the world.

Champions League
European club competition held every year. The winner is the best team in Europe.

Premier League
The top football league in England.

Serie A
The top football league in Italy.

La Liga
The top football league in Spain.

Major League Soccer (MLS)
The top football league in the USA.

Euros
European Championship, Europe's main national team competition.

HAVE YOU READ ANY OF THESE OTHER BOOKS FROM THE SUPERSTARS SERIES?

FOOTBALL SUPERSTARS

COLLECT THEM ALL!

SPORTS SUPERSTARS

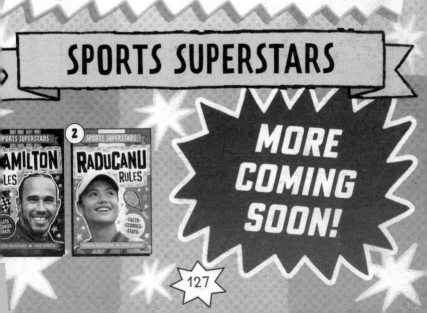

MORE COMING SOON!

ABOUT THE AUTHORS

Simon's first job was at the Science Museum, making paper aeroplanes and blowing bubbles big enough for your dad to stand in. Since then he's written all sorts of books about the stuff he likes, from dinosaurs and rockets, to llamas, loud music and of course, football. Simon has supported Ipswich Town since they won the FA Cup in 1978 (it's true - look it up) and once sat next to Rio Ferdinand on a train. He lives in Kent with his wife and daughter, a dog and a cat.

Dan has drawn silly pictures since he could hold a crayon. Then he grew up and started making books about stuff like trucks, space, people's jobs, *Doctor Who* and *Star Wars*. Dan remembers Ipswich Town winning the FA Cup but he didn't watch it because he was too busy making a Viking ship out of brown paper. As a result, he knows more about Vikings than football. Dan lives in Suffolk with his wife, son, daughter and a dog that takes him for very long walks.